T0303661

More Praise for
The Horse Eaters

"*The Horse Eaters* is a masterful blending of a resilience blueprint, wisdom for the poetic journey into justice, and artfully divine inspiration. How does one negotiate life when given the tools of negativity but the inner spirit houses an abundance of gifted determination? Dr. Nzinga writes, 'If you have a bulldozer; you can wait for opportunity. If you have a teaspoon; you must learn to make it.' *The Horse Eaters* beautifully displays the notions of searching for freedom inside of a given storm, and pulls no punches in regard to the harshness of the traverse. But, it also delivers a road map, lined with prophetic clarity, on how to survive a systemic trampling. The words are not simply to be read. They are to be ingested and worn upon the heart."

– REGINA EVANS, Bay Area entrepreneur, performer, playwright, and owner of Regina's Door in Downtown, Oakland

The Horse Eaters

Ayodele Nzinga

NOMADIC PRESS

OAKLAND
111 FAIRMOUNT AVENUE
OAKLAND, CA 94611

BROOKLYN
475 KENT AVENUE #302
BROOKLYN, NY 11249

WWW.NOMADICPRESS.ORG

MASTHEAD
FOUNDING AND MANAGING EDITOR
J. K. FOWLER

ASSOCIATE EDITOR
MICHAELA MULLIN

DESIGN
J. K. FOWLER

COMMUNITY EDITOR
TONGO EISEN-MARTIN

MISSION STATEMENT
Nomadic Press is a 501 (C)(3) not-for-profit organization that supports the works of emerging and established writers and artists. Through publications (including translations) and performances, Nomadic Press aims to build community among artists and across disciplines.

SUBMISSIONS
Nomadic Press wholeheartedly accepts unsolicited book manuscripts. To submit your work, please visit www.nomadicpress.org/submissions

DISTRIBUTION
Orders by trade bookstores and wholesalers:
Small Press Distribution,
1341 Seventh Street
Berkeley, CA 94701
spd@spdbooks.org
(510) 524-1668 / (800) 869-7553

The Horse Eaters
© 2017 by Ayodele Nzinga

This book was made possible by a loving community of chosen family and friends, old and new.

For author questions or to book a reading at your bookstore, university/school, or alternative establishment, please send an email to info@nomadicpress.org.

Cover and back artwork by Arthur Johnstone

Published by Nomadic Press, 111 Fairmount Avenue, Oakland, CA 94611

Third printing, 2019

Printed in the United States of America

LIBRARY OF CONGRESS CATALOGING-IN-PUBLICATION DATA

Nzinga, Ayodele 1952 –
Title: *The Horse Eaters*
P. CM.
Summary: This is an origin tale, a reclamation of memory, a movement towards wholeness in thought that helps shape action and inform deed. These poems are an anchor cast out from the graveyard in the Atlantic ocean tethering the beginning of the myth of me in North America to a place.

[1.BLACK HISTORY. 2. POETRY/LOVE. 3. AMERICAN GENERAL.] I. III. TITLE.

2017955974

ISBN: 978-0-9994471-4-7

The Horse Eaters

Ayodele Nzinga

NOMADIC
PRESS

Dedicated to those who stayed the path rocks and all to give me today. It honors those who took the path they opened, those they left behind in the known, those unknown to me in the unknown wilderness of this SorrowLand, and the bones in the Atlantic Ocean the world's largest graveyard.

CONTENTS

THE PARABLE OF
BULLDOZERS AND TEASPOONS

IN THE LAND OF milk and honey there are people who are born with bulldozers. They have inheritances, family businesses, old money, and connections—they will always land on their feet. Even the crooked among them, will be righted, there is less impetus to play fairly if you were born with a bulldozer—you simply arrange things to your liking. Then there are those, who like me, are not born with bulldozers; they are born in debt, wading in cycles that want breaking, and burdened by trauma that goes untreated. These people are born with teaspoons. I was born with a teaspoon, so I am not without tools.

I am the descendant of horse eaters, intimately familiar, with the sharp tart taste of equine flesh. A meat that does not "taste like chicken," or beef, with a smell all its own. I learned on the road, in search of myself, that poor North American African farmers who managed to own the scraps of land they farmed, were loathed to be reduced to the position of sharecroppers.

The sharecroppers fate was the quintessential essence of impossible. They worked land owned by others in exchange for the privilege of living on that land, and being able to farm a small portion for themselves. Given the worst plots of land, they reentered servitude, forced to purchase everything necessary to work the land from the company store. The Company store would run a tab for the sharecroppers who lived in a pauper like state of perpetual debt.

By contrast, poor land owners would do all they could to ensure they were not indebted at the end of a harvest. If a harvest failed, and the leanest of winter threaten to consume them, rather than accrue debt, they would eat their livestock—right down to the horses. They had a teaspoon and they used it to insure the land stayed free.

I am the seed of dungeons, dank passages of no return; my ancestors came to this shore fettered by chains in the bottom of ships, and we have spent centuries trying to dig our collective self out of the hole we have been cast into. We are locked in competition with those born with bulldozers for our share in the dream of America. A dream we helped to construct, our blood watered the roots, is poured into the foundation, but armed with teaspoons, we have had difficulty obtaining a share, let alone our fair share. As inequity grows steadily in North America, and around the globe, those armed only with teaspoons may feel that it impossible to ever find even ground. Systemic racism coupled with naked hubris fuels invisible narratives, whose tentacles seek to constrain even the possibility of flourishing. In some homes, those with teaspoons dine mostly on hope. That hope is precious.

Snared in the framework, of a system that oppresses us for being, by its very being; we must learn to define wealth, health, and progress for ourselves. We have no time to pay attention to shiny things destined for landfills, rather, it is our duty to invest in self and other's born with teaspoons. We are a set, coded as such by color, social position, and the invisible line of class stratification. North American Africans are a new tribe, born of enslaved Africans on American shores, we have a common trauma, a common history, and are systemically locked in the bottom of the boat 400 years after the ending of chattel slavery in America. We come to the table hobbled and delicate fearing the day when "the call" comes that reminds us we were born with teaspoons.

The intellect, fortitude, and sheer will it took to coalesce purposely decimated, shredded, and diverse cultures into something new and serviceable in a SorrowLand, while forging ground upon which to stand existentially, is without parallel in recorded history.

Those with teaspoons have been and must continue to be tireless. No time for distractions or becoming mired in the wrong conversations. Self-pity is useless. Anger is good fuel but it will eventually burn you out. Persistence is a necessity as is self-determination. Self-love and generosity of spirit are essential, these things will feed and sustain you. One must have a firm grasp on their own reality—they must by necessity become authors of their own fate.

There is a narrative offered for those born beyond the pale. If you are born with a teaspoon and are going somewhere in life, you will need to clear that narrative from your path. The narrative offered for you says; you are less than able, you lack drive, morals, have no work ethic, no aesthetic, no aspiration, you are not worthy. This narrative also colors you as dangerous, possibly criminal, anti-intellectual, and the ultimate other, the antithesis of what is good, right, proper, and worthy. If you accept for a moment the boundaries implied in the narrative crafted for you, precious time that could be spent in using your teaspoon to its best advantage, will be lost due to your lack of clarity. The will of a thousand with teaspoons outweighs the will of one with a bulldozer.

If you have a bulldozer; you can wait for opportunity. If you have a teaspoon, you must learn to make it. If you have a bulldozer, you can roll over obstacles on the way to your destination. If you have a teaspoon, you need to find a way to dismantle obstacles, go around them, or turn them to your purpose. If you have a bulldozer, you can afford sloth because you are well fed. If you have a teaspoon, you are probably hungry. Some journeys take generations. Be careful about what you leave for others to build with. Create what you need as you clear your path. Keep your hands, and that teaspoon, moving. Pray because you are grateful for the teaspoon and hands—but keep your hands moving while you pray.

HUNGER

The Babalawo said:
if the grandfather is a hustler
the son will be a businessman
the grandson will be a beggar.
i am the hunger
refusing to beg on the road
i build roads to other places
hands moving prayerfully
creating what's needed moving
forward on the path walking
where others will not holding
broken things on my way to
the ocean where dreams
sink swim or drown there is
no crown but there is bread
crowns are heavy
bread can be shared
sometimes
the road disappears
we must begin again
uphill with a bucket of water
that's got a hole in it
add a stone to plug the hole
on we go singing in the storm
the child of horse eaters
praying even ground
before the boneyard

THE QUESTION

can you keep your
shoulder to the wheel
you can't see turning
knowing the harvest is
not for you dressed in flesh
you will reap in the grave
the future you feed may
never feed you
the horse eaters land is gone
the children sold it to
go to the city
their dreams needed
cement would not
grow in the soil
full of rocks and promise
becoming became a
thorn in the basket
life offered they
wanted meat with
the sweet potatoes
the horse eaters
held on to the land
to feed the future's dream of itself
will you
continue to till the soil
for tomorrows trees
can you see over today's
demands that tomorrow
will starve without seeds
it demands you point the
way out of no way
clear the path leave the map
see yourself as a cartographer
for things to come growing

out of you needing a place to
stand in the world clear the
mine field so the future can
go forward use a teaspoon
if that's all you have
some ate horses
to clear the road
for what came after
those who came before
what is coming will
stand on your shoulders
lift your head
empty yourself of all you
were given all you dream
all you are so that they
remember to honor hunger
because hunger calls forth
the honor of labor singing
who you are in the world
what you give the future
how you cleared the path
so that they keep
shoulders to the wheel
is the story of
what comes next

JUBA FOR THE TEASPOON

there are things you know
inside without being told
the soul remembers it knows
intimately overstanding
things stuffed into the darkest
parts of closets
tucked in darker closets
what we push down forget
in order to breathe
you know things
that are not a question
fire bearing witness
scorching
embossed inside knowing like
the scent of flowers
you
could choose to follow
to the root we are our parent's children
they theirs and again backwards to the
reasons
the ways
the means the path
chosen the one way up that defined
what out could look like the places
where the road forked
the blood split skin broken
the hustlin' builders
those who squandered ease
the beggars left on the roadside
the lions the sheep the warriors
the scoundrels the heroic and some not so
the lost things on the way the found ground
the sound of the song reverberating
waiting

for your part of it the place you pick up
responsibility that may one day turn to blame
or the myth of lifting the bridge to
breath in your lungs the narrow space
of now in which you must certainly know
you shape what can be after as
firmly as it was shaped for you
will you be forgotten or remembered
will you be the vibration
the slap on the skin
or the drum major
a way maker
steadfast
as the horse eaters
determined to go forward
like waves rising corn growing trees
worshipping dog stars
what does the bottom of the ocean demand
what do the bones you stand on
scream for are you
blade or weed
hunger
or the breeder of beggars
a climber of mountains
who forgets
the valley or a bag of feathers folded
into glittering vain folly
waste of a dream dreamed
by those who refused to fail
held your place in the storm
claimed your survival
wrote it on today
like a deed to life carved
into a rocky hillside

one rusted teaspoon at a time
in a land of bulldozers

SIRIUS BLUE COSMOLOGY

there was a time we
watched the skies from
a different point in the universe
seeing even the ones
that were invisible
to naked eyes unanointed
usurpers usurping usurped us
cotton came
we crossed over feeding the
graveyard to serve
cotton sugar indigo
like scattered universes pulled
from orbit by an arbitrary god
that we could not know
we came forth
spitting out the eaters of horses
into the storm
blistered rebellious scorned
sore from bondage
bent spirits never bowed
unbroken planting themselves
on the side of a hill
praying life out of it
holding on to it with bleeding
fingers rubbing hope
between calloused palms
breathing out a future
that would be taller
go further went farther
sold the land
went to the city
got degrees
that said they (we) know
should have held on to the land

now landless in the city
where the ground is melting
dispersing the dispersed
where what (you) we know
is not what (we) you need
having forgotten what (you) we
should have remembered
larger stars
tales from
the graveyard indigo sugar
and good old cotton
you find yourself
in the wrong conversations
hugging the wind that
won't blow for you
consumed by hunger
fermented into thirst
no horses to eat here
on the avenues
oozing cracked lives
composting broken promises
in hallow shadows of
debts due
no horses mules
no acres of land
what's left to be
manifest in the eye
of the whirlwind
how will tomorrow
eat how will we
survive the day
live past this minute
if we refuse to snatch
the thunder sing

the lightening
like a prayer call
be the force
that drives the storm
by any means
calling forth the morning after
the road cleared
for the of tale the future
served like a guest at a full table
rooted as firmly
oak redwood
evergreen
faithful
as the horse eaters
imagined in frozen-out-of-life winters
looking over barren fields
sharpening machetes
to clear our path

WIND

last night i intended to
dream of the horse eaters
standing stoically
against the wind
i dreamed instead
the wind
chafing my thoughts of
going forward
tenderly carrying calloused
dreams of locomotion
demanding translation
loosely layered over
real rude reality rubbing
out today's music in
the dark silences
made scripture by devotion
the wind howling pushing
blowing a dirty blue ditty
eating the foam off the ocean
crying in the key of old Godz
screaming remember
i woke shivering
wind playing with
the curtain in the window
recalling dreams of flight
grateful for the wind

THE HORSE EATERS' CHILDREN

                    i can only go back
                    three generations
                ten generations are your
                  pantheon of ancestors
                i am short six generations
                    i only go forward
                  maybe one day i will go
                  back across to the other
                side of the graveyard in the
                    ocean if my soul
                    can ever leave the
              water but only if i go forward
                  i only know forward
            i am the child of the horse eaters
                  that's where i begin as far
                back as i can go to the farm
              where my grandmother took me
              when my mother left me after
              traveling down route 66 she
              stopped to give birth migrated
          a wingless southern bird learned to fly
                she left singing freedom bluz
                    looking for new music
                        leaving my
                        grandmother
                    the girl from the farm
                        on the
                        side of a hill
                        to claim me
                        before
                    we went looking
                        for her
              traveling like unopened promises
                  in the colored car on the

train clacking across the country
traveling to fate
with lunch in grease stained bags we
went to the horse eaters
frozen into the middle of a skinny winter
near my birthday
christmas some winter month filled with
unrepentant snow
packed tight on hard ground
i remember presents a car coat
red in my memory
store bought
warm with a hood
a hand carved
rocking chair
bell ringing when i rocked
bell and chair
left behind
we took the car coat
hood on my head my face on
the train window steamed with
my breath we clacked away
from the land gone
from the horse eaters
i wonder what happened to the chair
i wonder what happened to the land
when the children left the horse eaters
the children became
teachers real estate agents
they became nurses
accountants they
went to the city
perhaps they sold the farm
spilt the dreams sweat prayers

of the horse eaters
into equal parts in pursuit
of their place in our song
of becoming
i was too little to know
but i remember-ed the
tart sharp taste of horse
flesh remember-ed the
smell of the simmering meat
not the horses
alive
so much but
the meal they made know now
the promise they held fed
more than hunger
in the body they fed hunger
in the soul
the possibility of becoming
nourished souls that survived
paper thin times absent milk
no honey
to go to the city
to be other things to be
more than the horse
eaters could dream
of tilling and sowing with
lean harvest following
lean harvest followed
by leaner harvest
with growing children with
dreams of the city when the snow is on the
ground all you have is what you have
when the house is tarred to keep out the wind
howling like an old lady turned out into the night

rooms going straight back shotgun style
devouring precious land that reluctantly yields
life but inside the house
life is abundant
as are dreams
the
the horse eaters are the children
of hunger
they have climbed a steep hill
learned to hold on
buried their hope in the
stones and dirt
dangling from the side of life
holding on
their children grow they
pour their love into them
holding on
you must hold on when life
wants to shake you out of it
hold on to what you
have if you want more
you must hold on to the land
wrested from blood sweat bottomless hope
on the steep side of the hill
you must hold on or
dreams starve
once the taxes are paid the tithes tithed
once the tools are
repaired the store is paid all the
too many bills are paid all
the labor spent is spent
hunger's dreams remain
when the land won't feed you
fights back refusing

to yield you must hold on
feed the dreams
the future has to eat
kill the livestock
all of it down to
the horses
feed the future's
dreams gravy
grits full bellies
land
that the future
will sell to
go to the
city
without the land
we ate
horses
to save

HORSE EATERS

born singing outside the graveyard
only a whisper away from
sharecropping
two generations up from cotton
no way home no way forward
the wandering tribe of the newly
freed owed nothing
owning nothing
determined to survive they struggled
forward in the storm the children
of the whirlwind walking on top
of the water head to the sky eating
the rain traveling with the thunder
swelling bellies
dirt under fingernails in nostrils
in communion with the dirt
ordered by the logic of the natural
speaking to the dust the wind
the memory of oceans
willing life
from rocky ground purchased an acre
at a time hands moving
labor sweat blood tears
bound in the shit piss the fear
of others
othered
by decree by deed by text by tortfeasors
the rancid taste of overcoming
bowing down to own more land
hoarding pennies
doing without to hold on
rock roughed soil
steepest part of the hill
slim to none better than nothing

work harder
pray with your hands moving building making
no quarter
just forward
daring to dream of something on the other
side knowing there was another side
before here
separated by the graveyard in the ocean
standing
in fire eyes on the horizon feet and soul
planted in the land
leaning on it pulling
the next day from it one slender blade at a
time if the harvest is good they will
be able to buy horses
to till more land to plant more
dreams for greater tomorrows they
endure the arduous labor of the day
pregnant with the future's expectations

CHILD OF THE HORSE EATERS

i am a horse eater
dungeon seed
pantheon divided
6/10's on the other side
razor sliced by water
untethered
4 generations
force fed to
doors of no return
after crossing
the graveyard in the ocean
i have not returned
in flesh
spirit is more stubborn
memory is everything
then it is more
it is life before life
illumination
in a time of dark lamps
a map leading you
a reason
the way out of no way
it is horse meat cooked
served thankfully eaten to hold on to
land sweated bled for
we ate the horses
we kept the land
teaspoons in a
land of bulldozers
we used our spoons
used stones to plug
the hole in the bucket
that was only half
full of water in the

first place we
grew out of the land
like promises tumbleweeds
on route 66 on trains west
looking for dreams
dreamers with teaspoons
carving the path they
walked on walking away
sometimes
when it melted sometimes
melting you with it
daring to fight sometimes
drawing razors straddling yellow lines
sometimes
able to rise
from the battle field
whole enough to know
how to win
sometimes wisdom is
stop fighting
taking the loss moving migrating
fleeing refugees with teaspoons
buckets with holes
the memory of the taste
of horse flesh pushing
forward with hope
on our breath

THE BALLAD OF THE
HORSE EATERS

singing in captivity
is not a sign of happy
slaves nor is dancing
which may occur almost anywhere
grace in the storm
may be hard to understand
may not always be seen as
divinity holding hands with resilience
what do you know
of laying burdens down
sitting them next to you in
a dark place losing their weight
to dance your story
sing it to a starless sky
with no moon
in language, you thought you had forgotten
to supplicate yourself to joy
thanking the Orisa for
strong backs
bottomless souls
sweetened with gratitude
knowing the burden waits
weighs the same may have
grown in your absence but
you are stronger now

singing while captive
does not imply happy
slaves nor does dancing
which may occur almost
anywhere

HORSE DAY

sun baked day
like any day
just a day
until it's a day
worth remembering
on a tedious tuesday
the horses came
two lean large eyed
looking hungry too
horses
two
prosperity after
hunger after want
after white light
bright blinded
almost erased
we can see now
what the hard ground
will yield when we
have more muscle
only as good as the tools
we use he used to say
pride in his dark eyes
leading thin horses
up a rocky hill
our horses
our hill
our chance
an extra hot water
cornbread day like
sunday on tuesday
celebration
signs of our right
to be lucky

to continue to struggle
to not drown
in the steadfastness of the storm
to continue performing
the miracle of
pulling
our skinny life from the dirt
the Godz sent horses
we will eat only
beans for a month
to pay for them
hallelujah Ase-O
pass the hot water
corn bread pour the last
of the syrup we fall down
to get up reaching
we go forward no chance
turned to slim chance
we dance juba thankful
for the promise
in the horses
we will fatten them
planting our hope in them
like the seeds we
will plant
in hopes of harvesting
more than ill will
rolling down more predictably than
the rain we pray
up in the heat of
deeply shined hunger
inside the inside
of our souls
praying

to rise like
the sparse shoots
that defy odds to
keep us just alive
enough to want more

two horses
lead by a slender rope
harnessing our future

MORNING

we grew out of the soil
from ancient coastal cities
with music in their names
we have forgotten
the names of the cities
the meaning of the rhythms
we traversed the unknown
unwillingly eaten by a thing
we would
come to know have
names for but that would come
later after
we learned to swim
without water to fly
without wings
to hold our breath
for centuries
praying for the morning
before
suffering lead us
to imagine locomotion
resurrection
after dying
out of
the known to the nothing
to boldly conjure life
in
death's dank belly
burning like forgotten stars
in the night
claim the body
dig the hole
in the
morning

gone
now spooked taken took
made holy ghost
invisible
walk without legs
climb by
instinct reclaiming
recreating
making new out
of scraps
sacred memory
necessity mothering survival
written in the blood
inking
the story of becoming
to overcome
still overcoming
standing
on broken things that
struggled to leave
enough to stand on
giving all and all
to the all and all of
going forward
knee deep in
nightmares
bloody leaves
successions of shallow graves
without markers
walking on water in
a storm
roaring through centuries of
trying to make it
to the morning

RUSTY BUCKET PROMISES

some days seem
like the best i ever
had is
a rusty bucket
half full of water with
a hole in it
on good days
i remember to be grateful
for the bucket
to be joy filled
that when i close my eyes
i always see the sky
jubilant because i found a stone
to stick in the hole and we drink
water all in all
i have learned to be tall
in the face of things that
have every intention of making me
small
uphill is ok i got feet
know how to pray with hands moving
been in the rain before know how
to make the sun shine how to make
my now better so i can make best
teaspoon in motion
eyes on the horizon
feet in the graveyard
growing out of yesterday
like a finger pointed skyward
errands for ancestors
turn to blessings
i got a teaspoon
a bucket
a stone

dreams older than me
more mountains
on the path
debts to collect
promises to keep
to those who
ate horses to make
sure that
i had a teaspoon

LONG-DISTANCE RUNNER

i never was a sprinter—
perhaps i wanted to be
bleached concrete
bright lights
places that wrap genius
in gaudy murder
for trying not to be invisible
called to me since age three.
But higher powers had a plan for me-
ancestors whispering
walk with great faith to your fate
that's your destiny.
See me—
i'm a long-distance runner
built to go the distance
not so much for speed.
The sleeper
natural late-blooming prodigy-
the three-orbed interlocutor
the hood's oracle
all eyes
intently set on eternities—
time has no meaning to me.
Who measures oceans
when their destiny
is to flow into
them like seas?
Thunder does not fear lightening.
i have come to Rumi's garden and
lingered to stroll beyond it
to an open field
of nuanced understanding.
i am a long-distance runner.
i have sat at the feet of my Baba

becoming
as North 'Merikan Afrikans
consumed by coerced evolution
studied revolutions in
China, Cuba, and Bolivia
as windows once open shattered
as doors slammed shut—
i witnessed the fall of
Camelot, a King, and a Shining Prince
as Panther's roared but were snared
in nappy nets as sons set
before fully rising.
Multiple murderers.
One hand buying all the bullets.
Nefariousness
draped in off the shoulder hubris
and a pale blue blonde dress.
i am a long-distance runner-
blood of conquering conjurers
Nat Turner Hannibal Queen Nzinga.
i walk a path worn smooth by
the makers of a way out of no way—
bowing only
before Godz
smuggled in the tight airless funk
of good ships
fit with shackles
the ocean wind all creation
melted to fit inside
the myth of a holy ghost
still favoring drums
the horse eaters, runaway slaves, those long-eyed boyz
glued to the sidewalk on city corners
running from the law even in still

moments folded between lynchings
and picnics
the preacher's wife and the coroner
All say Ashe
to the path makers
guardians of the seasons
sunrise birth death sunset
keepers of eternities
owning the wind
real rainmakers
the line that winds back to
the beginning of time-
i am without beginning or end.
i am built to go the distance—
not so much for speed.
Time has little meaning
when you are looking at the sky
from above
upper rooms where alchemist
tinker with surety
to author impossible destiny
prismatic overstanding
hexing my oppression
time is a silk thread
on which i am a bead
strung in a succession
of beautiful beads
each a life—
a world
hanging from the neck
of the Godz true love.
Multiple verses in a sonnet
being re-membered by the multi-verse.
i remember when there were

no astronomers only
Dog Star people who
re-membered the invisible.
Nommo resurrectus explicit
I am
Before time was time
naked chaos surrendered to the
ritual of living word
I am
what i say
I am
by the breath in my lungs
the tip of my tongue
a creator of galaxies
and my reality
let there be light to explore the sublimity
of inky black darkness
perfection perfected
personified
speaking invisible
to visible
sewing together those
dispersed like chafe
seeding a Diaspora
without a tongue.
Thank the Godz for drums-
beating the time of hearts
un-captured waiting time
our feet learned to speak
the unspeakable
dancing on oppression
we are dangerous
daring to be us
when in rhythm.

Without drum wisdom
in the madness of
right now
the machete
is the only song
left in the box of crusted lies
the antidote
the cure
we could sing here now
right here right now
loud and off-key outside and othered
where blood speaks
to blood calling blood
blood answers
are you waiting for the album?
Long distance runner
driven by vision-
i re-member dancers
warriors dipping fluid frames
breaking time as shields clash
with dreams as alien as the dreamers-
the builders of fences
turning fireworks into guns
trafficking cocaine opium rum
sickness madness death
since they come—
dividing poisoning ravenous omnivores
under one flag
cross bones and currency
pale-eyed true believers
with a long view—
time has no meaning
if your name is
dynasty oligarchy institutional-whiteness

script writers unfurling
distortions of reality in 3D—
see believe follow
or
be the vibration of the drum
watch the horizon for that
long distance runner
oblivious to time
constant as the tide
in possession of persistence
built to go the distance
not so much for speed.
Done gone digital
mega global
maximizing the local
counting strands of resistance
numbered like stars in
countless constellations.
Long distance runner dreams
one struggle one nation one direction
ever forward
cross borders
many tongues
new dances
air broken by
militant fists
and a million lips
proclaiming
disdain of denials
de-conjuring the constraints
not asking
taking reparations
agents of change
cyber drums

aligned in the chaos
flash micro-revolutions
fade the ever evolution
may the way makers will be done.
All say
no band aids
just solutions.
An eye on the prize
kind a ride
pushing the pendulum
with every stride
creating the vortex
we travel in
the eye of the whirlwind
running viral across airwaves
invisible – tremble
if we become indivisible.
I re-member when
music was invisible—
crossing Jordan
charting by the North Star
movement got us this far
swing down chariot
dreams of 'Trane still wanna
ride in memory of Miles
Pullman porters and losses
to other folk's wars.
We still water
running through the blues
marching the gospel of loco-motives
we got dreams
dreams of distance
growing from blood stained trees.
We got funk soaked aspirations

realities carved at the high cost
of constant resistance.
Who can be well in sickness?
Much time fighting —
need more time building
destruction is means not end —
disruption is only the forward to
the book of what comes next
we need new dances
got to stay
limber in this limbo
of post-colonial smelting
stewing in this pot of post racism.
Form a second line
and fearlessly cheer
without fear of time
that has always had its own mind
in a world that has forever been
full of clear and present danger.
Kidnappers
lawless thugs authoring law
guilty
stealing continents
soiling the air
leveling mountains
to build condos out of oversized egos
compensating for lack that creates
unquenchable thirst in anemic slivers of soul—
Claim the time for a second wind
you can savor the journey
if you are sure of the inheritance
new music
the constancy of drummers drumming
and long-distance runners
that come to run.

CLEAR

i am awake
wide eyed sure
aware here inside
conscious looking
out from knowing
no rose-colored glasses
clear unafraid clear
sure here present in this
moment with real wounds
transformed into myths of honor
worn like a crown
debts paid in charge of deciding
where the line is and who can
cross over owning my want
suffering anger and hope
memories of wars won wars
lost the cost of all born warrior
no separation from my protection
the Godz whisper
the dead translate
i listen
my swords cut both ways
dessert eagles stop
doves and hawks from crying
always fit for battle
all battles are not fit
to be fought some are to
be understood others
to fit you for bigger battles
some to bleed you of intention
never bleed without gaining ground
there is no romance in suffering
struggle bleeds early graves
not fame

the cost of owning want is heavy
as is struggling not to want
choose your battles
i have learned
to see farther down the road than
looking like the distance
between hearing
understanding and pushing back
the wind knows when not to blow
when to be a hurricane
when to push the water over
the shore when to fan the fire
I am unseparated from
my knowing
collard greens buttermilk cornbread
sweet potato if you lucky
someone else's
land house school city
country dream freedom justice wealth
progress forward movement manufacturing
the manifestation
of rites over others rights
the right to other others
all the juice boxes in your lunch box
your daddy own the water fountain
your grandfather patented water
poverty smells like fried chicken in
small rooms with windows painted
shut no gardens liquor stores 3 strikes
eviction profiling jail cells
drug addiction too small shoes the
word no and dried blood
i understand the way words flip
flop like dead fish playing dead

like landmines hidden in the dirt
lurking in the funk of being
alive painting reality sometimes
using the N visible crayon
singing colorblind anthems
broadcast onto reality
making it hard to under
stand really real hard to
separate it from the mesmerizing
bitty bopp spit by the system
humming while you dream
working while you pray
eating your shadow until
you are not sure if you
are real anymore
i am here
eyes wide
seeing
beyond looking
understanding beyond hearing
like the distance between knowing
and pushing back

PROMISE

hands raw from work
dedicated to writing their future
carving a space for tomorrow
to stand with rusted teaspoons
in a land of bulldozers
tenderly caressing the
unborn future
sowing possibility
in the impossibility of winters
that refuse to end assured
spring will come walking in
faith because faith grows inside
even when nothing else will
expecting needing wanting
the future to remember
the wind at its back
wanting it to go forward
willing to stand still
fighting so that it can
stand still

WIND WALKER

the wind at your back
wraps your coat around you
pushes you forward or
lays you low the wind
is ever at your back
it will not rest so you
cannot time spilling
all the right now
right here there is
on the road
behind the wind
the sound of it
howling snapping
a belt tightening
miles to go
task for the ancestors
food for the future
the gift for the
present
the wind at your back

ACKNOWLEDGEMENTS

"The Parable of Teaspoons and Bulldozer" was published in a longer form by *Vision Magazine* in June 2015 commemorating the 20th year of Juneteenth in Berkeley, California. "Long Distance Runner" has appeared in a different version in self-published work.

Special thanks to Tongo Eisen-Martin, a wordsmith's wordsmith. I wish you eternal fiyah and infinite flow.

One Word, One Struggle,

One,

WordSlanger

AYODELE NZINGA

When I was little my mother asked me what I wanted to be and then told me that it was impossible. She knew there was a story already written for me. I didn't like that story. I did not listen to it, so it never had a chance to limit me, I am the horse eater's child, with eyes for tomorrow. I write my reality. I am in love with the power of words and the way they hide their role in creating reality. Strung together, words create narratives— whole worlds live inside the words, multiverses reside within the stories they compose. I am a writer drunk off story painting my world with words as the medium. I make theater and plot the trajectory of tomorrow from West Oakland, California, the center of my artistic universe, where I live with a tribe of unlikely magicians who only go forward.